CREATURES OF THE WILD

MOOSE

GENERAL EDITOR:
JAMES M. PEEK
DEPARTMENT OF FISH & WILDLIFE RESOURCES, UNIVERSITY OF IDAHO

PHOTOGRAPHY BY
CRAIG AND ROBIN BRANDT

CHARTWELL
BOOKS, INC.

This edition first published in 1998 by
PRC Publishing Ltd.
Kiln House,
210 New Kings Road,
London SW6 4NZ

© 1998 Promotional Reprint Company Ltd.

CHARTWELL BOOKS INC.
A division of BOOK SALES, INC

114 Northfield Avenue

Edison, New Jersey 08837

This edition was produced by American Graphic Systems, Inc., in cooperation with the
Northwest Natural History Society (NWNHS)
Design © 1998 American Graphic Systems, Inc.
Designed and captioned by Bill Yenne

All photographs are © 1998 Craig and Robin Brandt

We are grateful for the information provided for this book by the US Fish & Wildlife Service

Note on terminology: According to the United States Endangered Species Act, the term "endangered" means a species is considered in danger of extinction throughout all or a significant portion of its range, while "threatened" is a less dire category, meaning a species is considered likely to become endangered, but not in danger of extinction.
The moose is categorized as neither threatened nor endangered.

ISBN 0 78580 8272

Printed and bound in China

MOOSE

GENERAL EDITOR:

JAMES M. PEEK

DEPARTMENT OF FISH & WILDLIFE RESOURCES,
UNIVERSITY OF IDAHO

For many people across the northern regions of this world, the moose (*Alces alces*) represents the major game species and a major part of the wildlife resource. Moose are among the most widely distributed of the world's large land mammals. They are thought to have evolved on the Eurasian continent, dispersing across the Bering land bridge during ancient times when the ocean retreated and exposed enough land to allow major interchange of mammals between continents. Indeed, some mammals moved back from North America to Asia across this bridge, and the big moose of the Chukotka region of Russia may be an example.

One of the rather amazing recent findings about moose is how genetically uniform they are across their range. While one might intuitively expect such a widely distributed mammal to have genetically differentiated itself, this species has the plasticity be able to adapt to the variety of habitats without much differentiation in genetic makeup. Evolution is thought to have occurred millennia ago for many of the large mammals, and this indeed appears to be the case for the moose.

Early in the twentieth century, North American *Alces alces* were subdivided into three groups. These were the American, or common, moose (*Alces ameri-*

canus americanus), indigenous to North America east of the Rockies, and the Shiras moose (*Alces americanus shirasi*), named for naturalist George Shiras III, and common to the Rockies, mainly north of Yellowstone National Park. The Alaska, or Kenai, moose, was then known as *Alces gigas* because the moose of that area are so much larger. All moose are now recognized as a single species, regardless of size. *Alces alces* is now subdivided into four primary subspecies in North America, with their identification based on the old early twentieth century idea of individual species. The largest subspecies, *Alces alces gigas* (formerly *Alces gigas*) ranges from northwestern British Columbia into western Yukon Territory and throughout most of Alaska.

The subspecies *Alces alces shirasi* can be found in western Wyoming, north and central Idaho, western Montana, southwestern Alberta, southeastern British Columbia, and in isolated areas of Utah, Colorado, and extreme northwestern Washington. It was originally most common in the

Opposite: A large bull moose browsing on willow and white spruce in a subarctic taiga forest in Alaska's Denali National Park.

MOOSE: PREFERRED FOREST HABITATS

Aspen	Grand fir	Red spruce - yellow birch
Balsam fir	Hemlock - yellow birch	Sitka spruce
Balsam poplar	Interior Douglas fir	Tamarack
Black cottonwood - willow	Limber pine	Western hemlock
Black spruce	Lodgepole pine	Western hemlock -
Black spruce - paper birch	Mountain hemlock	Sitka spruce
Black spruce - tamarack	Northern white cedar	Western larch
Blue spruce	Pacific Douglas fir	Western red cedar -
Coastal true fir - hemlock	Paper birch	Western hemlock
Cottonwood - willow	Paper birch - red spruce -	Western red cedar
Douglas fir - western hemlock	balsam fir	Western white pine
Eastern hemlock	Pin cherry	White pine - hemlock
Eastern white pine	Red alder	White spruce
Engelmann spruce - subalpine fir	Red pine	White spruce - aspen
	Red spruce	White spruce - paper birch
	Red spruce - balsam fir	Whitebark pine

Yellowstone regions of Montana and Wyoming, but has been expanding its range in those two states and becoming more common in Idaho, Utah, and Washington. It has now been successfully introduced into Colorado, and is also now considered to be the subspecies that occurs in the East Kootenay region of British Columbia and adjacent southwestern Alberta. Suffice to say that the moose has been able to adjust successfully to contemporary conditions where human influence is increasing on its range.

The subspecies *Alces alces andersoni* ranges from northern Minnesota, Wisconsin, and Michigan into western Ontario, west to central British Columbia, and north to eastern Yukon Territory and the Northwest Territories. The subspecies *Alces alces americana* ranges from Maine and Nova Scotia, west through Quebec and central Ontario, and from Hudson Bay south to the Great Lakes. In Maine, where moose hunting was banned from 1935 to 1980, the subspecies has become especially abundant. It is estimated that the moose population in northern Maine increased from about 7,000 in 1950 to more than 20,000 by 1990 and that their range is spreading into adjacent states. By the 1990s, moose were being reported as far south as Connecticut for the first time in many decades.

In Europe, *Alces alces* is known as the "elk," which is not to be confused with the North American wapiti (*Cervus elaphus*), which is also known as the elk. The Eastern Hemisphere contains three subspecies of moose, with one of the smallest subspecies being the most widely distributed across Scandinavia,

Opposite: A cow moose feeding in the Chena River near Fairbanks, Alaska. Such moose eat all types of aquatic plants, such as water lilies, pondweed, horsetails and bladderworts.

FAMILY CERVIDAE ADULT WEIGHT COMPARISONS
Pounds (Kilograms in parentheses)

Moose (*Alces alces*)		
	Low average	800(360)
	High average	1,300(580)
White-tailed (Virginia) deer (*Odocoileus virginianus*)		
	Low average	150(70)
	High average	300(140)
Mule (black-tailed) deer (*Odocoileus hemionus*)		
	Low average	150(70)
	High average	400(180)
Elk (wapiti) (*Cervus elaphus*)		
	Low average	500(230)
	High average	1,000(450)
Caribou(*Rangifer tarandus*)		
	Low average	220(100)
	High average	300(140)

Lithuania, Latvia, Estonia, Poland, Germany, and the northwestern parts of Russia. Another smaller subspecies occurs in northern China and southeastern Russia. These may have a higher percentage of non-palmated antlers than other subspecies. The big moose of northeastern Russia approaches the size of the Alaska-Yukon subspecies in North America. Antlers of these big animals may be wider than six feet, longer than four feet, and have weight upward of 75 pounds, with multiple brow tines and many tines off of the main palms.

Moose began to expand their range across the three continents in the 1940s and 1950s. Photographs were taken of moose walking across an airport in Russia in the 1950s. Moose have expanded their range to the Arctic Ocean in both Canada and Alaska over the past half-century. This colonization is still occurring, with moose beginning to appear in portions of north-central Idaho, where they were never seen before the late 1980s. The reasons for this continued expansion range from better protection from human exploitation and creation of suitable habitat. In the far north, where moose colonize the narrow shrub communities along the river systems, perhaps reduced predation at intervals facilitates the colonization.

Toward the southern portions of the extant range, combinations of forest maturation, which provide protective cover during the hottest portions of the year. Logging, which has created shrub fields, may be responsible for the expansion. Hunters have often misidentified moose for elk, and as they have become more aware of the presence of moose, the inadvertent loss of moose

Opposite: A pair of battling bull moose. Such a contest may involve a few hits with both combatants walking away, or it may heat up into a fight to the death.

FAMILY CERVIDAE ADULT HEIGHT COMPARISONS
Inches (centimeters in parentheses) measured at shoulders

Moose (*Alces alces*)

Low average	78(195)
High average	84(210)

White-tailed (Virginia) deer (*Odocoileus virginianus*)

Low average	36(90)
High average	42(110)

Mule (black-tailed) deer (*Odocoileus hemionus*)

Low average	36(90)
High average	42(110)

Elk (wapiti) (*Cervus elaphus*)

Low average	40(100)
High average	60(150)

Caribou(*Rangifer tarandus*)

Low average	40(100)
High average	48(120)

during elk hunting seasons has diminished. Probably the moose, being adapted to the cold continental climate, is limited by heat in summer on the southern portions of its habitat, where sickness and mortality during the summer has been noted.

THE MOOSE SOCIAL SYSTEM

A mature bull moose will weigh from one-fourth to one-third more than a mature cow. Adults of the largest subspecies may weigh up to 2,000 pounds, and the smaller subspecies 1,000 pounds. At the peak of its annual prime, the rutting bull may virtually cease to eat in order to devote full time to breeding activities, and during the month of rutting may lose a one-fourth of its body weight. The rut peaks around the first of October, and dissipates by the second week of that month to where bulls may again congregate with each other in areas of high forage supplies to gain reserves for the oncoming winter. The cow never ceases to feed during the rut and continues its quest for nutrition in accordance with the annual fluctuations in forage availability and quality.

The moose is commonly thought to be the least gregarious of the antlered game, but this is a misleading generality. Probably the most fixed social group is the nuclear unit of cow and calves. The calves, born around the first of June, are able to follow the protective cow almost immediately after they are

Opposite: A cow moose photographed in the rich light of the afternoon sun.

FAMILY CERVIDAE ADULT LENGTH COMPARISONS
Inches (centimeters in parentheses)

Moose (*Alces alces*)		
	Low average	72(180)
	High average	96(240)
White-tailed (Virginia) deer (*Odocoileus virginianus*)		
	Low average	54(135)
	High average	84(210)
Mule (black-tailed) deer (*Odocoileus hemionus*)		
	Low average	48(120)
	High average	80(200)
Elk (wapiti) (*Cervus elaphus*)		
	Low average	64(160)
	High average	100(270)
Caribou(*Rangifer tarandus*)		
	Low average	54(135)
	High average	84(210)

born, so they depend primarily upon their mother and her abilities to protect them from wolves and bears. Cows with calves are not the least bit gregarious, but bulls may be found socializing in loose groups, usually of less than five, during the summer. Groups of bulls in these loose aggregations again coalesce in late fall, where up to 15 or 20 animals may congregate in the same area.

Winter aggregations depend upon the terrain. The open shrub-scrub communities of central Alaska and the Yukon promote aggregations of cows, calves and younger bulls. The winter grounds in Quebec allow closer associations of moose which benefit from the trails they create in the deep, heavy snows. The river bottoms of the West may serve as sources of concentrated forage for aggregations that are forced into these bottoms by the deeper snows and scarcer forage supplies on the mountains. In midwinter, one may find two or three mature bulls moving

Above: Alaska is home to several important moose populations, including the Kenai Peninsula, the Seward Peninsula and the area, seen here, in and around Denali National Park.

Opposite: An excellent portrait of a bull moose with massive, 12-point antlers.

around together, aloof of one another but still in close proximity. The presence of more than one bull probably facilitates early detection of predators. Aggregations are also dependent upon density of the population: higher densities promote more apparent socialization. Even in the least social of antlered species, changes in sociability are apparent throughout the year and among the sexes and age classes.

Above: A bull moose grazing in the thick underbrush.

PRODUCTIVITY

Earlier observers considered the moose a very unproductive animal because they relied on observations by forest workers to supply their information. Then in the 1950s studies in Alaska, British Columbia and Newfoundland revealed that the moose was similar in

Above: Moose are easily distinguished from other deer through their huge, long, overhanging snout and throat with its "bell," a flap of skin covered with long hair.

reproductive capability to the mule deer: Yearlings were able to breed, adults could produce twins and occasionally triplets, and an individual could breed and produce young each year. The variations seen from one population to another could be explained by the quality and quantity of the forage base. Also, cows with calves were found to be very reclusive and less visible to the observer in the field than cows without calves or bulls. Predation, where wolves and bears occur, also accounts for lost calves, especially where the cow must defend two.

The question as to why twinning occurs among moose probably lies in the origins of the species in the boreal forest. Moose habitat is transitional in nature, because the important species of plants on which the browse thrive in forest openings created by wildfire and wind. Low density populations of moose persist in mature forest along the riparian zones adjacent to lakes and streams, and then individuals are able to disperse

Above: Their extremely long legs (sometimes up to 40 inches) make moose appear somewhat awkward. Despite their appearance, moose are not ponderous and can move quickly.

Opposite: A bull moose.

to newly created habitats. The calves stay with the cow through their first winter, but are repelled if the cow bears another calf during the following spring. Even if the cow does not bear calves, a yearling bull will be ejected from the family circle during the following autumn rut. He then begins a dispersal that may eventually lead him into newly created habitat.

Older animals which have established ranges are not likely to disperse, but the younger ones, which are in the process of acquiring a range, will move. Thus the proclivity to produce twins and to disperse may be characteristics of moose that help them to find and proliferate in newly created habitats in the boreal forest. This tendency to disperse also explains why moose are often located in unexpected places, such as a wheat field far away from occupied moose habitat, or on the outskirts of a town equally far removed from their traditional range.

Above: The antlers of the bull moose — such as pictured here — are shed seasonally. During growth, these are covered with skin called velvet, which dies and is rubbed off when the antlers reach full size.

Above: A bull moose "in velvet." Between August and September, the velvet is rubbed off the antlers by grinding and sharpening them on trees. This will give the antlers polished look.

THE RUTTING SEASON

The antlers of the moose, along with the bell or dewlap, characterize the species. Both are considered "social organs," important in the intricate behavior patterns that confer dominance and subordination. Likely, the evolution of the species in boreal forest may be responsible for the side-oriented displays and the broad, palmate antlers. In the shrub fields and dense forest the more frontal displays more typical of the elk may be less effective than the broadside displays. When two competing bulls approach each other in the rut, broadside displays, where the full size of the animal is best observed, are common. The bull slowly moves its head up and down, further emphasizing the antlers. The bell, longest on the older bulls (unless it freezes off, as it may at the higher latitudes) further emphasizes the size of the individual.

Above and opposite: The cow moose is slightly smaller than the bull, and has no antlers.

If the broadside display does not suffice, then the two bulls may engage in a "parallel walk," to further size each other up. If all else fails, a fight then occurs, with the two participants pushing each other with their antlers, straining to gain an extra footing and to cause the opponent to break off the fight, or slip. These fights may end in serious injury to one or both participants. Mortality also occurs on occasion, illustrating that the contests for mates is energy-consuming and a major natural selection process for males.

Fights may be distinguished from sparring matches, which occur between bulls of different sizes. A big, mature bull may tolerate the vigorous sparring of a yearling, for instance, without responding any more than necessary to catch the smaller antlers. These sparring matches probably serve to provide fighting experience for the younger animal, and perhaps as refreshers for the older bulls.

Above: In September and October, during the fall rutting season, bulls engage in sparring matches with other males, using their giant antlers to assert their dominance and win favor with the cow that is a prospective mate.

Above: The bull that wins in battle with a competing bull, will soon begin the courtship of the favored cow. The moose mating season occurs during September through October.

The rutting pit is a part of the breeding ritual that has been investigated for its significance. The bull, and sometimes the cow, paws out a moist site and urinates in it and lies down in it. This presumably enhances the olfactory aspects of the rut. This activity is also observed in the elk (wapiti) and is akin to the "scrape" that the white-tail buck produces. During all of this activity, the cow moose, which is the center of attention, is usually placidly feeding nearby, apparently oblivious to the contest. When there are reasonable numbers of males around, the cow may be somewhat selective in who she allows to mate with her. This may not always be the largest bull with the biggest antlers the winner of the fights. Fighting skill and experience have something to do with who wins, and who gets the female.

Moose are classified as polygamous, meaning that one male may mate with more than one female during the rut. In boreal forests and in

Above and opposite: A cow moose and her newborn calf. For calving, cows need dense cover bordering younger stands which provide substantial food.

the Western states, a bull will typically sequester a single female at a time. However, in the vast, open habitat that is found in central Alaska and Yukon Territory, females will form into a group during the rutting season, with one bull attempting to sequester all of them. These groups are similar to the harems typical of the elk, but are more loosely organized and so they are not considered to be harems.

Bulls are usually physically capable of breeding as yearlings, but they may not, and there are two factors which may prevent them from doing so. First, the cow may reject the advances of the immature suitor in favor of the more experienced bull, and second, the older bulls may prevent the yearling from participating. However, in populations where adult bulls have been seriously diminished through hunting or natural causes attributable to high mortality during severe winters, the yearlings then may become more important as breeders.

Above and opposite: A newborn moose calf struggles to his feet to take his first tentative steps.

If the rut is a major natural selective agent for the bull, then the ability of the cow to produce a calf which survives to breeding age is important for the female sex. This ability relates to how well the cow sustains herself through the winter when forage is naturally lean and of low nutritive value, how many calves may be produced, and how well they survive.

Nutrition is related to the condition in which the cow finds herself at the beginning of the winter, how abundant the forage supplies are during the winter, the length of the winter and what kind of forage supplies will be available between the end of the winter and the calving season. The abundance of forage involves not only the amount of forage supplies themselves, but also the number of moose that are feeding on those supplies. Overall nutrition is relative to population density as well as to forage condition.

Above and opposite: A cow moose licks her newborn calf as his sister awaits her turn. Twins occur frequently if females receive more than adequate nutrition.

PREDATORS

Predator attacks mark the major cause of mortality accruing to calves, and most such attacks occur in the summer when the calf is weakest. While the cow is a ferocious opponent for a wolf or a bear, persistence and opportunity eventually favor the predator. An experienced cow will better protect the calf or calves, and the predator may not press the attack if the cow is perceived to be a serious threat.

Moose are not easy prey and are able to defend themselves against even the most determined of predators. For example, wolves that feed primarily on moose are known to incur broken bones and abrasions, evidence of the effectiveness of the adult in protecting itself and the calf. Predation may also be more apparent when environmental conditions cause the prey base to be more vulnerable, as during and after a severe

Above: A wary mother takes her calf to the stream to drink. As is exhibited in the behavior pattern illustrated here, the cow moose are very protective of their young.

Above: Moose calves, usually with their mothers for at least a year after birth, make the transition from nursing to browsing by observing the feeding behavior of the cow.

winter. Also, when a population is at high density, it may provide more vulnerable individuals for the predator to locate and kill.

While wolves, which hunt in packs that can overwhelm a moose, are the primary non-human predator, both black bears and grizzly bears may also be effective predators when conditions allow. Some individual bears learn to prey upon adult bulls after the rut, when they are weakened. In this way, the moose will serve as a source of protein for the bear just before it enters the winter den for hibernation. While hunters are the major cause of mortality in areas where hunting occurs, in their absence, most moose probably die through predation, malnutrition, or rutting-associated causes.

Typically, calves are most vulnerable and suffer the most mortality, and the probability of surviving increases as the individual becomes an adult. Then, as the adult — especially a bull — reaches older ages, it

Above and opposite: As the moose calf develops during the first summer of life, it begins to take on the physical characteristics of an adult. These include the humped shoulders and the coloration on her face. Not yet evident in the calf seen here, the distinctive shape of the head and snout will develop within the first year.

becomes more vulnerable to mortality factors, including hunting. Because the older bull may also have the largest antlers, a hunter is more likely to go after him, rather than a cow of any age. However, even in the absence of hunting, the female is more apt to survive to an older age than the male, as is the case with many mammals.

Above and opposite: A cow moose in an Alaskan pond. Such moose are observed to use bogs and other aquatic areas more frequently in the summer than in the autumn or spring.

DISEASES AND PARASITES

I n the moose's eastern range, the brain worm parasite called *Parelaphostrongylus tenuis* occasionally causes substantial mortality. This parasite causes blindness, disorientation, paralysis and eventually death in moose. Larvae that have climbed onto leaves of twigs are ingested as the moose browses, and they migrate through the animal to

the meningeal tissues along the spinal chord and into the brain. The *Parelaphostrongylus tenuis* parasite is indigenous to white-tailed deer, which are somehow able to tolerate its presence. In areas where deer and moose coexist, the brain worm becomes an important mortality factor to moose.

In the Maritime Provinces of eastern Canada, moose are more likely able to winter at higher elevations or in deeper snows than white-tailed deer. This is seen as a direct consequence of the presence of *Parelaphostrongylus tenuis*. Thus, what is described by naturalists as a "tension zone" exists on the southern ranges where the moose and white-tailed deer coexist year-round.

During favorable weather periods, white-tails may be able to occupy more northerly regions than during periods when deeper snows persist. When white-tails move north into the moose range, the incidence of

Above and opposite: A cow moose and her maturing calf. In the summer, moose can be found in open areas near water where forage is abundant. In the past, wildlife biologists have assumed that clear-cuts were beneficial to moose because such cuts favor abundant growth of the plants moose browse on. However, it has been ascertained that moose need at least some cover during every season and usually will not venture into large, open areas with no cover.

parasitism may be expected to increase in moose. The situation may be influenced by habitat conditions which favor deer over moose as well. Logging and other land use practices which enhance deer habitat can aggravate the problem.

Other diseases and parasites may contribute to reduced ability of individuals to cope with predators and severe winters. The winter tick can cause significant hair loss in late winter and early spring. The liver fluke, which requires a canine alternate host to complete its life cycle, can cause significant liver damage, which also contributes to mortality. Typically, diseases and parasites contribute to the deterioration of the individual and become important to overall populations when periods of forage scarcity or high density concentrations predispose the moose to poorer conditions. During years when forage supplies are adequate, animals are better able to tolerate disease and parasites.

Above: A bull moose lumbering through deep snow. During the winter, such moose prefer forested areas and move into denser, conifer-dominated forests as the winter progresses. In mountainous areas of the West, moose have been observed to concentrate at elevations below 3,500 feet during the winter.

Above: Two bull moose, their new antlers still in velvet, on a mountainside rich with brush. During the summer, moose move to higher elevations, usually above 5,000 feet.

LONGEVITY

Just how old does a moose get? They are capable of living beyond 20 years, but perhaps a better and more appropriate question is "just *when* does a moose become old?" One answer may be found in the wear upon the teeth. A moose obtains its adult set of teeth at about 19 months of age, close to the age when a white-tailed deer does. The first permanent tooth, erupting shortly after birth, is the first molar. That molar finally wears smooth on its grinding surface at between eight and nine years, although there will be individual variation. So perhaps when that molar becomes smooth is the time when the individual may be classified as "senior."

The moose's teeth reveal much about the life of an individual. Some moose will exhibit grooved incisors when twigs have been stripped in a

Above: A cow moose browsing. A moose's home range varies from 100 square miles in Alaska to between eight and 15 square miles in northeastern North America.

Opposite: A cow moose eating aquatic plants. Such vegetation constitutes a high percentage of moose subsistence.

habitual manner, while others show even wear. Others will show uneven wear patterns, where the opposing tooth will be offset or longer, or missing.

Diseases may cause the decay of a tooth, leading to its loss and, eventually, to erosion of the dentary bone. A moose with dental anomalies may well be a candidate for predation or winter mortality so they don't live as long. Also, the high crowns, and early replacement of milk dentition with adult dentition, are adaptations to the woody plants that moose typically browse upon. It should be noted that woody plants and leaves are less erosive than the grasses that elk and other cervid species graze upon, so tooth wear is actually slower in the moose than in the elk. An elk replaces its milk teeth completely by three years of age, as compared to a year and a half for the moose, but, on average, both show smooth molars at the same age.

Above and opposite: Cow moose browsing. Throughout their range in North America, moose most commonly browse on birch, cottonwood, willow, aspen, and balsam fir. They often consume serviceberry, mountain ash, honeysuckle and dogwood. Moose also eat various species of mushrooms, grasses, lichens and sarsaparilla.

FOOD HABITS

Willows constitute the major forage source for moose across most of their range. The taller willows often are preferred over the shorter ones, although virtually all species are eaten. In boreal forests, where willows may be scarce, other species such as maples, cherries, aspens, service berries, mountain ash, yews, and balsam fir may be important. On Western ranges, willow bottoms provide important forage sources, and dogwood appears to be especially palatable. Douglas fir and subalpine fir substitute for the balsam fir on Western ranges. Moose in the North feed primarily on deciduous browse all year, with no palatable conifers as alternative forage.

Grasses are not used substantially, but forbs, the flowering, broadleaf, succulent plants that dry up and die back each season, may be

Above: a bull moose makes his presence known. As with elk, moose have a distinctive call that is used for long distance communication.

Opposite: A young two-spike bull moose.

highly preferred in some areas. Sticky geranium and the cinquefoils have been observed to receive heavy use in southwestern Montana.

Aquatic feeding is commonly observed wherever moose and ponds or rivers occur together. Pond weeds and lilies are favored aquatic foods. Reasons for moose favoring aquatic plants include their high sodium content, their high digestibility, and the fact that they are associated with water, which the moose spend time in because it serves as protection from insects that are so prevalent in much of moose country (although the peak of use by moose does not necessarily coincide with the peak insect abundance, and there are alternate sources of sodium in the form of licks in many parts of the moose range). Also, moose thrive in areas where alternate sources of sodium are scarce, whether in the form of aquatic plants or mineral waters. Probably the high digestibility of aquatic plants, which contain high percentages of water, is the prima-

Above: A cow moose and her calves drinking from a stream. In Alaska and northern Canada, moose have been observed to move to stream bottoms as winter approaches to take advantage of taller willow species used for food and cut banks used for shelter from the wind.

Above: Moose distribution in winter is limited by the availability of woody food plants and by snow conditions, such as its depth, density, hardness, and duration.

ry reason for their use. Moose will submerge entirely to feed on pond weeds, with records of dives to 20 feet below the surface in Ontario lakes. Moose are adept swimmers, and may be seen crossing large bodies of water. In the 1920s, moose swam 22 miles across Lake Superior to Isle Royale to successfully colonize that island.

Moose appear to develop feeding preferences, with certain foods being eaten extensively by some and not by others in the same area. This is probably the result of learning what to eat, which occurs early in life when the moose is still associated with its dam, as well as to what is available and palatable within the region. A mature moose may ingest up to 40 pounds of forage on a daily basis during the summer, but as palatable plants shed their leaves, the amount of forage ingested will decline. In midwinter, moose become relatively inactive and feeding times decrease to annual lows. The animal enters an energy conservation mode

Above and opposite: Moose need a variety of habitats, from dense, coniferous forests to more open, aquatic areas with some cover.

in keeping with the season of scarcity, moving little, interacting with other moose less, using the heavier cover, spending more time bedded and chewing the cud. During this period of scarcity, forage preferences are considerably subordinated to whatever is available, but even then preferences can be detected.

MOVEMENTS AND HOME RANGE

Moose exhibit highly variable movement patterns, both across their range and through the annual cycle of seasons. Large-scale movements of hundreds of miles are recorded for the Russian taiga moose, even when terrain is not very variable. In North America, moose on the eastern portions of their range are not as migra-

Above and opposite: Biologists have calculated that the optimal moose winter range is composed of conifers taller than 18 feet, with a canopy closure of 75 percent or greater. Cover becomes critical during severe winters in areas where snow depth exceeds 40 inches, because at these depths moose can't move about easily.

tory as are the ones occupying more mountainous terrain. Migrations are probably related to where the best forage supplies exist at the time. While the willow bottom along a river system or lakes at the lower elevations constitute the typical winter range for Shiras moose, they may shift into the adjacent parks, aspen stands and sparse conifers as the forage base proliferates and becomes available in spring. In summer, a variety of habitats may be used, but often the higher drainages, associated shrub stands, and moist meadows are preferred. These areas remain occupied through the rut, after which an upward movement may take place in early winter. When snows deepen, a downward movement towards the lower willow bottoms occurs. In some areas where the riparian zones containing willows do not exist, moose may remain high all winter, moving from one tree well to another and existing on the scant forage protruding beneath the trees and the trees themselves.

Above: In the winter, moose in the Clearwater River drainage of Idaho have been observed to inhabit dense stands of evergreens characterized by subalpine fir, with Pacific yew as the primary underbrush and their preferred forage.

Above: A cow moose and her calf. Bull moose are solitary except
during breeding season, while the cows usually travel with their
calves until the latter are about a year old.

In Wells Gray Provincial Park, British Columbia, the moose that undertake the altitudinal migrations appear to be more productive than moose that remain at the lower elevations yearlong. There appears to be an advantage in migrating, probably related to access to the most nutritious forage, as it continues to appear later at the higher elevations.

Home ranges are highly variable in size, shape, and between seasons and years. In Denali National Park and Preserve, home ranges for two bulls for one winter were 2,100 acres and 4,990 acres, respectively, when the entire area they circumscribed with their travel was calculated. However, in actuality, the bulls used specific areas intensively within the home range, traveling between these areas and spending little time in transit. The same pattern of home range use, wherein highly preferred locations receive the bulk of the use and the rest of the area receives much lower use, appears to be typical. This suggests that a moose views

Above: A cow moose swimming a stream. Moose are powerful swimmers, and have been observed to swim as fast as two people can paddle a canoe.

Above: In national parks such as Yellowstone, Grand Teton, Glacier, Banff, Jasper, Isle Royale or Denali, moose can often be seen in or near shallow ponds, streams or marshes close to forests.

its habitat as a series of patches, and knows where the best parts of it are for feeding and resting.

An interesting home range pattern has been detected in Denali National Park and Preserve for some mature bull moose. The summer and winter range are separated, which is not unexpected, but a separate rutting area is also used. The bulls will move to this rutting area some time in late August or early September and remain there through the breeding season. Bulls attempt to sequester the cows that cross their rutting areas, but will not search after them if they move out of the area. Rutting areas may be established relative to locations of other bulls, and be retained on a basis of dominance over peers. This is not well understood, except that it obviously confers breeding advantages to the bull or it wouldn't exist.

Above: The moose's antlers are shed between November and January, and, as seen here, they begin to grow back in the spring.

Above: A bull moose photographed at dawn in September, his new antlers still covered in velvet. Moose are often active in the late evening, but may be observed at any time of the day.

RELATIONS WITH HUMANS

O ne does not want to venture close to a young calf because the cow is highly protective of it. The cow defends itself and her calf by striking with the front hooves. An angry cow lowers its head, raised the hackles across its shoulders, lowers its ears, and finally charges the source of irritation. This is the defense against highly aggressive predators that is most effective, and it can be used against other intruders as well.

It has been noted that the bulls in rut are less likely to be threatening. Indeed, the big bulls in Alaska's Denali National Park seem interested only in other bulls and other cows during the rut, and can be approached to close distances without being provoked. However, the recorded death of a person who got too close to a moose wintering in

Above: A bull moose with a full rack partially rubbed clear of velvet.

Above: A cow moose rubbing herself on a small white spruce as she browses on a sapling. Rubbing is often seen as a sign of a female's "mating readiness" during rutting season.

Anchorage, Alaska, illustrates that the animals may become highly irritable during winter and quite intolerant of humans. It is not uncommon for moose to be seen in the suburbs of Alaskan and Canadian cities.

Each year, there are many reports from Maine to Alaska of moose attacking vehicles on highways, and there are many cases of people being chased up a tree or indoors by a moose. Whether the animal was deliberately chasing the person, just being curious, or mistook the person for a predator or another moose is uncertain.

In most cases, moose are more apt to flee from humans than to approach or threaten them, but if an moose is surprised at close quarters and feels threatened, it may retaliate. The best policy is to remain a distance from any moose, as a matter of common sense and respect for the animal.

Above: A cow and her calf feeding in a pond. In the warm months, moose feed on water plants, such as water lilies, pondweed and horsetails. In the winter, they browse on conifers and eat their needles.

Above: A cow sheltering her calf who is nursing, shoulder-deep in a pond. The cow moose jealously guard their offspring and often react violently if they think the calf is being threatened.

ECOLOGY AND MANAGEMENT

The moose, being the largest herbivore in the boreal forests it occupies. Thus, in an ecological context, it may be considered a keystone species, meaning that it has an important influence upon its habitat, and therefore upon the habitat of a variety of other species. Moose contribute to the redistribution and recycling of nutrients through their browsing.

Detailed studies of moose have been undertaken at Isle Royale National Park because this population is contained within the ecosystem of the 572,000-acre island, which represents a sort of microcosm of moose habitat in the upper Great Lakes area of the United States and Canada. Investigations have focused both on the moose and their predators.

Above: A bull moose charging. Moose move swiftly on land and some have been clocked at 35 miles per hour.

Opposite: The bull moose is particularly aggressive during the rutting season.

Studies of moose feeding habits illustrate that browsing pressures influence plant species composition and even soil characteristics. The abundance of aquatic plants in the ponds and lakes of Isle Royale, as well as the distribution of yew, have been considerably diminished.

Isle Royale's unique environment has also been useful in looking at predators. Wolves have been present as moose predators since they migrated here across the frozen surface of the lake in 1949. Their numbers, relative to the moose population, have gone through some interesting fluctuations. For three decades, the numbers of wolves increased, and the number of moose declined, especially in the 1970s, when deep snow for several succeeding winters made the moose population particularly vulnerable. However, with the lessened snowfall generally experienced in the 1980s, the Isle Royale wolf population declined dramatically, and the moose population increased to about 1,500. This number, as interpreted by some nat-

Above and opposite: Moose are not truly nocturnal, but they are frequently active at night. Because of this, they will often sleep in the daytime, as this one has been doing. Among large animals, some, such as horses, sleep standing up, but moose will lie down to sleep.

uralists, may actually too strong and too healthy for the wolves to kill enough to ensure their own survival.

In the context of moose habitat, alteration of aspen communities by moose has been documented in Alaska and Montana, and most certainly productivity of willows in the riparian zones is affected. However, browsing pressures below some levels actually may increase productivity, while sustained, severe browsing may cause plant production to eventually decline.

The ever-fluctuating environment in these areas means that moose do not browse any specific plant with the same frequency and intensity each year, a reason for the perpetuation of the forage base. The presence of predators also causes the animals to shift, creating changes in browse use. Moose densities must be quite high before the extreme changes in the environment as recorded on Isle Royale will occur.

Above: When bulls are in rut, as is this one, they utter a series of deep grunts that, although they don't seem to be loud, are so deep that they can be heard over long distances.

Opposite: A cow moose responds to the call of a bull.

In Scandinavia and Russia, damage to conifers by moose through heavy browsing is a source of concern among foresters and landowners who manage the forests for their commercial value. Populations must be maintained at levels which do not cause extensive damage if at all possible in such circumstances.

In the big national parks of North America — such as Denali, Banff, Jasper, Yellowstone and Glacier — where moose occur, their populations will continue to be allowed to fluctuate without overt human interference. In most of North America, moose are hunted under regulations which are designed to ensure that populations are maintained at levels suitable for the prevailing conditions of the region.

Moose are influenced by a highly fluctuating habitat over most of their range, and disturbances of the forests are needed to maintain substantial populations. Because much of the boreal forest that forms this

Above and opposite: A cow moose during early winter, at the end of mating season. It spring, she will probably give birth to a calf or two.

habitat is subject to logging, it is necessary to coordinate forest management with moose habitat management. Logging practices, which create openings in which shrubs predominate for a period of time and provide suitable habitat for moose, can be spaced in size and time throughout an area to benefit moose. In other areas, prescribed fire may be used to create openings or retain habitat in high quality condition. However, some portion of mature forest is also important to moose as well, so forest practices which provide for retention of older stands can also be important.

In the Rocky Mountain West, the highly important riparian zones are subject to flooding, river channel changes, and corresponding alterations in the willow communities upon which they depend. Some managers of these areas will use prescribed fire to reduce decadent, out-of-reach willows. However, moose will also benefit from the retention of willow communities in the riparian zones. In portions of the Idaho

Above and opposite: A bull moose amid deep mid-winter snows.

moose range, where riparian communities are unimportant as moose habitat — and mature forests are — logging practices which perpetuate retention of critical moose winter range (and which provide for its replacement when logging is deemed necessary) are considered to be desirable.

Only in the more northerly portions of their range are the habitats on which moose depend relatively stable, but the highly variable nature of the winters mean that in these regions snows may substitute for plant succession as major habitat fluctuations. These communities are not subject to wildfire and their management is basically one of ensuring their persistence.

Today, the moose seems to be relatively secure. Its habitat needs can be effectively coordinated in boreal forests which are also managed for their timber values. The important riparian zones which it thrives in are

Above and opposite: A bull moose during the mating season. In Maine, the moose population has grown, and it is now expanding to adjacent states.

increasingly recognized as being highly valuable for a variety of reasons, which helps to ensure their retention.

Human exploitation across much of its range is sufficiently regulated to ensure that over-harvests are minimized and correctable. Further, it is highly prized as a game species, which further helps perpetuate it. However, as the human population changes, or as the needs for forest products intensifies, then moose habitat may be lost, and there are examples across their range of this happening.

Ultimately, as with all wildlife, moose are dependent upon the whims of humans for their existence. We have enough knowledge to manage and maintain populations and habitat, and our ability to use that knowledge to sustain the species over the ages is the ultimate challenge.

Above: A bull moose amid characteristic browse species.

Above: The velvet will often hang on bull moose's antlers for some time before it is rubbed off completely to reveal the bull's rack of antlers.

Above: This bull is an excellent illustration of the fact that as a bull moose grows older, its antlers will generally grow larger and larger, and they will increase in the number of points they have.

Above: This intriguing view shows a spruce forest that has been used by a bull moose — or several bull moose — to scrape the velvet from their antlers.

Above and opposite: This bull moose, with one of the spikes of his antler broken, bears testimony to the ferocity of the battles fought by bulls during the rutting season. Within a month, however, the antler will drop off, and in spring it will grow back, larger than before.

INDEX